LIFE-SIZE
SHARKS
and other
UNDERWATER CREATURES

WRITTEN BY
DANIEL GILPIN

ILLUSTRATED BY
MARTIN KNOWELDEN

STERLING PUBLISHING CO., INC.
NEW YORK

First published in the UK in 2005 by
Chrysalis Children's Books,
an imprint of Chrysalis Books Group plc

Library of Congress Cataloging-in-Publication
Data Available

10 9 8 7 6 5 4 3 2 1

Published in 2005 by Sterling Publishing Co., Inc.
387 Park Avenue South, New York, NY 10016

Distributed in Canada by Sterling Publishing
c/o Canadian Manda Group,
165 Dufferin Street
Toronto, Ontario, Canada M6K 3H6

Associate Publisher Sarah Bertram
Project Editor Tom Jackson
Illustration Martin Knowelden
Designer Alix Wood

Picture acknowledgement:
1 Royalty Free/ Digital Vision
36TR The Art Archive/ Biblioteca Nazionale
Marciana Venice/ Dagli Orti

Sterling ISBN 1-4027-2537-X

Contents

Voyages of discovery

Most of the ocean is still unexplored. Many of the creatures that live down there have never been seen by human eyes. Each time scientists send submarines into the deep sea, they are going on voyages of discovery. New types of animal are being found there all the time, and some of them are very strange indeed.

In 2001, a new type of squid was discovered, with giant fins and stiff arms that stick out like the spokes of a bicycle wheel. Two years later, a weird type of armored snail covered in plates made of iron minerals was found.

Black-banded sea krait

The Life-size stamp

This stamp shows which sharks and other underwater creatures are illustrated as life size in this book. It's just as surprising to see how tiny things are, like the seahorse on this page, as to see how big they are. It's not possible to show all the creatures life size—the blue whale on page 12 is so big that its eye would barely fit into one page of this book! When creatures are not shown life size, a hand print, or human diver is included to give a sense of scale.

The deadly black-banded sea krait spends most of its time in warm water around coral reefs. Its tail is flattened to make a paddle. Sea kraits often slither onto land to lay eggs, find mates and to warm up in the sunshine.

5

WHAT LIVES UNDERWATER?

Water covers more than two thirds of our planet. Almost all of it is contained in the world's oceans and seas, and a huge number of animals live underwater. Some are familiar to most of us, but many are little known and hardly ever seen.

Fish and other vertebrates

Vertebrates are animals that have backbones, like us. Fish are vertebrates, and so are mammals and reptiles. Most underwater vertebrates are fish. Unlike mammals and reptiles, which must breathe air, fish breathe by removing oxygen from the water using organs called gills. More than 27,500 species (types) of fish have been discovered so far. They range in size from the tiny, ⅓-inch (9 mm) long dwarf goby to the whale shark, which can reach 59 feet (18 m) long.

Mammals that live underwater include seals, whales and dolphins. Underwater reptiles include turtles, crocodiles and sea snakes.

Seahorses must be some of the most unusual-looking fish. They feed on tiny floating animals, which they suck in through their tube-shaped mouths.

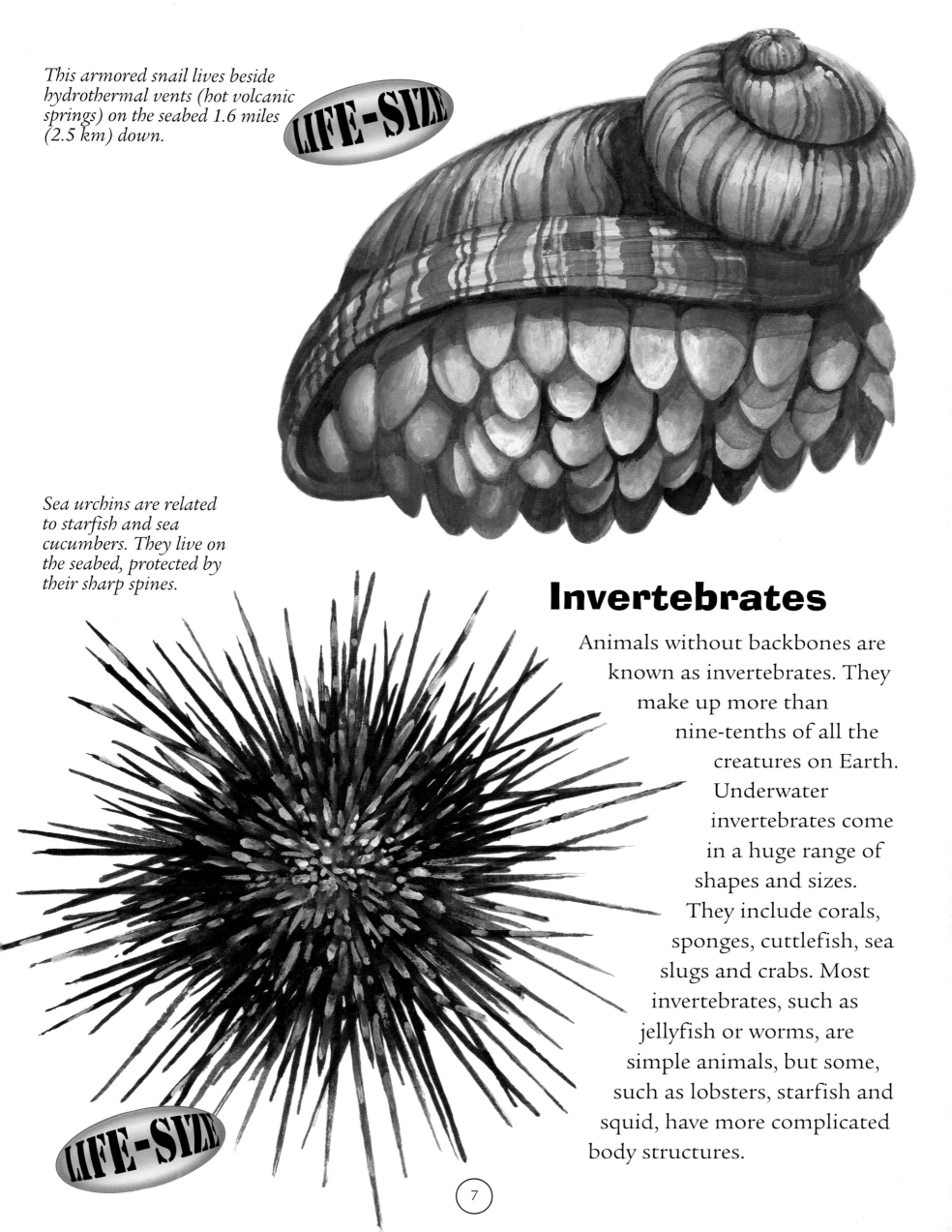

This armored snail lives beside hydrothermal vents (hot volcanic springs) on the seabed 1.6 miles (2.5 km) down.

LIFE-SIZE

Sea urchins are related to starfish and sea cucumbers. They live on the seabed, protected by their sharp spines.

Invertebrates

Animals without backbones are known as invertebrates. They make up more than nine-tenths of all the creatures on Earth. Underwater invertebrates come in a huge range of shapes and sizes. They include corals, sponges, cuttlefish, sea slugs and crabs. Most invertebrates, such as jellyfish or worms, are simple animals, but some, such as lobsters, starfish and squid, have more complicated body structures.

LIFE-SIZE

UNDER THE ICE

Much of the ocean around the North and South Poles is covered by ice. The creatures that live under it have to be especially tough to survive, yet large numbers manage to do so, including the world's biggest whales.

Krill

The most common animals in Antarctic waters (around the South Pole) are krill. These shrimplike creatures feed on tiny plantlike algae, which grow on the ice and in the sea itself. In spring and summer, krill form vast swarms, containing millions of individuals. Scientists think that there are around five hundred thousand billion krill in the oceans. That means that for every person on the planet there are more than eighty thousand krill! Krill are extremely important animals in the Antarctic, as they are eaten by almost all of the larger creatures that live there, from penguins to whales.

Krill may live for up to six years, if they can escape being eaten.

LIFE-SIZE

Arctic whales

In summer, the Arctic Ocean is full of whales. Many kinds, such as humpbacks and grey whales, swim up from seas farther south to feed on the huge shoals of fish that appear in the Arctic at this time of year.

A few types of whale spend their whole lives in the Arctic Ocean. They include the bowhead whale, a 100-tonne (110-ton) giant that has the biggest mouth of any animal on Earth – fully open, it could swallow a minibus! More common residents include the smaller beluga whale and narwhal.

Narwal

Beluga

Bowhead

These three species live in Arctic waters all year round.

Coping with cold

The sea creatures that live around the Arctic and Antarctic have different ways of dealing with the cold. Most air-breathing animals, such as whales, have a thick layer of fat just beneath the skin. This layer, known as blubber, acts like a blanket, keeping their body heat in.

Unlike whales, fish do not have blubber. Instead, they let their bodies get very cold. Polar fish save energy by being less active than fish in warmer waters. They don't get eaten because predatory fish are less active, too. However, hot-blooded, air-breathing animals, such as seals and penguins, find it easy to catch them!

LIFE-SIZE

Many polar fish have special adaptations to help them survive. For instance, the Antarctic ice fish has a natural antifreeze in its blood to prevent it freezing up.

LIFE-SIZE

Greenland shark

The Arctic Ocean (around the North Pole) has its own terrifying predator—the Greenland, or sleeper, shark. At 21 feet (6.5 m) long, this monster is the world's fourth largest shark—only the whale shark, basking shark and great white shark are bigger. Drifting along slowly to save its energy, the sleeper shark bursts into action when it sights prey. It eats almost anything, from fast-moving salmon to the flesh of dead whales. One Greenland shark was even found to have a whole reindeer in its stomach!

OCEAN GIANTS

The seas are home to the planet's biggest creatures. Animals can grow much larger here than on land because the water supports their bodies. Whales, the largest creatures of all, are mammals and must breathe air.

Filter-feeders

The world's biggest animals have enormous appetites. But rather than hunt other large animals, most eat huge amounts of much smaller prey. The world's three biggest whales—the blue whale, fin whale and bowhead—all feed on fish or krill. They gulp great mouthfuls of sea water filled with their tiny prey. The whales then filter this water through comblike curtains called baleen plates that line their mouths. Other giant filter-feeders, such as whale sharks and manta rays, eat even smaller sea life, known as plankton. They use their gills to sieve this food from the water.

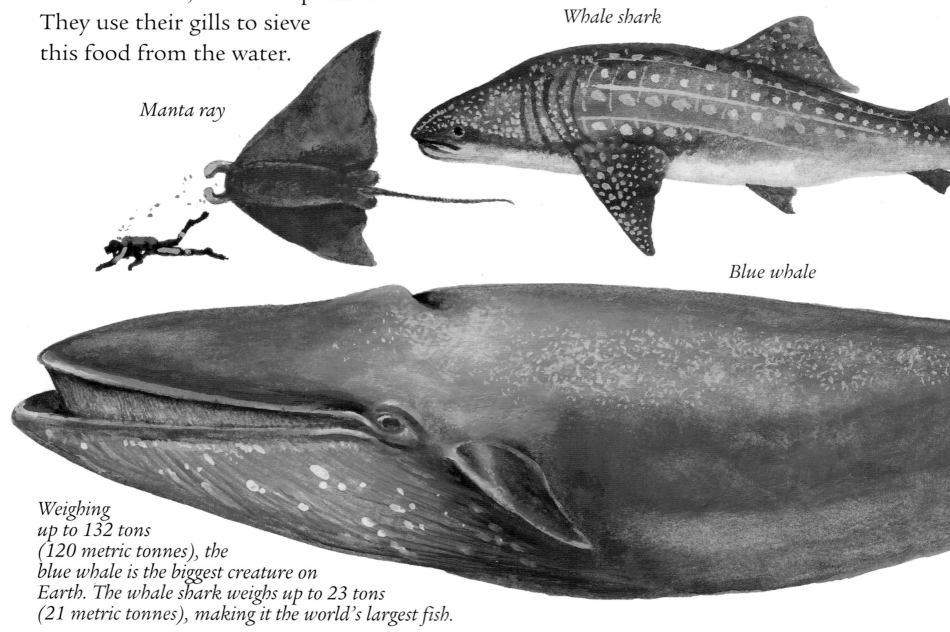

Manta ray

Whale shark

Blue whale

Weighing up to 132 tons (120 metric tonnes), the blue whale is the biggest creature on Earth. The whale shark weighs up to 23 tons (21 metric tonnes), making it the world's largest fish.

Cooperative killers

The killer whale is one of the most ferocious animals in the ocean. It hunts and kills all sorts of prey, including the blue whale and other creatures bigger than itself. Killer whales live and travel in family groups. They are highly intelligent and often work together to catch their food. Adult male killer whales can grow up to 27 feet (8 m) long and weigh 10 tons (9 metric tonnes). The females are smaller, usually reaching about 20 feet (6 m) long and weighing less than 6 ½ tons (6 metric tonnes).

The giant squid may weigh up to 2 ⅕ tons (2 metric tonnes), but it is little match for a 55-ton (50 metric tonnes) sperm whale.

The world's biggest predator

Although most of the world's great whales feed on small prey, there is one that takes on animals nearer its own size. The sperm whale is the world's fifth largest animal and its favorite food is another monster, the giant squid.

Sperm whales can dive to enormous depths. Occasionally, they may swim down as far as 2 miles (3 km) beneath the surface in search of prey. Sperm whales must hold their breath for an extremely long time, sometimes spending two hours underwater before coming up for air.

JAWS OF DEATH

The sea's most dangerous creatures can kill with a single bite. Sharks bite chunks from their prey, so that it quickly bleeds to death. They attack suddenly, powering into their victims before they have time to react.

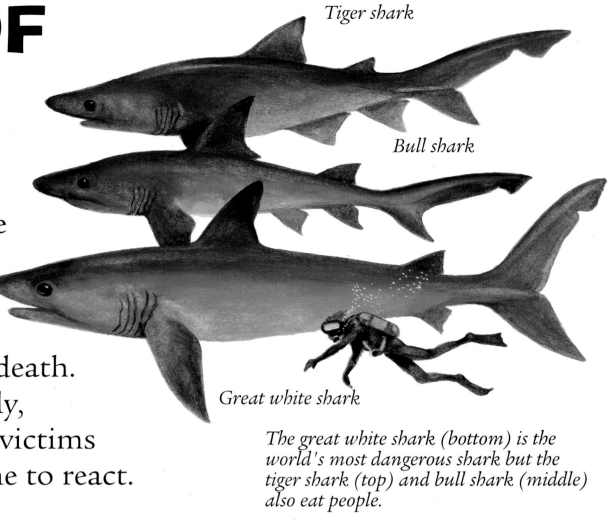

Tiger shark

Bull shark

Great white shark

The great white shark (bottom) is the world's most dangerous shark but the tiger shark (top) and bull shark (middle) also eat people.

Man-eating sharks

Most sharks are harmless but some kill and eat people! The most fearsome of all sharks is the great white. Its usual prey are seals but on a few occasions it mistakes swimmers or surfers for food. More than 250 people have been attacked by great white sharks over the last few hundred years, and nearly 70 have been killed. Other man-eaters include the tiger shark, bull shark, requiem shark and shortfin mako. In all, sharks attack about 100 people every year, and about a quarter of their victims die.

LIFE-SIZE

A new set of gnashers

Sharks are constantly growing new teeth. As old ones come loose or wear out, they are replaced by a new, sharper set behind them. Sharks use their teeth for slicing and ripping up flesh. Some may get through as many as 25,000 in a lifetime.

Fearsome fish

It is not just sharks that attack humans. All sorts of other fish can give a nasty bite if they feel threatened. One of the worst reputations belongs to the barracuda. This fast-moving predator usually keeps its distance but might turn on divers that have chased it or drifted too close.

The moray eel is another fish with a fierce reputation. It lives in warm seas and grows to 10 feet (3 m) long. By day, it hides in cracks and crevices among coral or rocks. If startled, it will lunge forward with its jaws open and bite anything that does not retreat.

Moray eels are fish with round snakelike bodies.

The barracuda is one of the most streamlined of all fish. When it swims, its body cuts through the water like a knife.

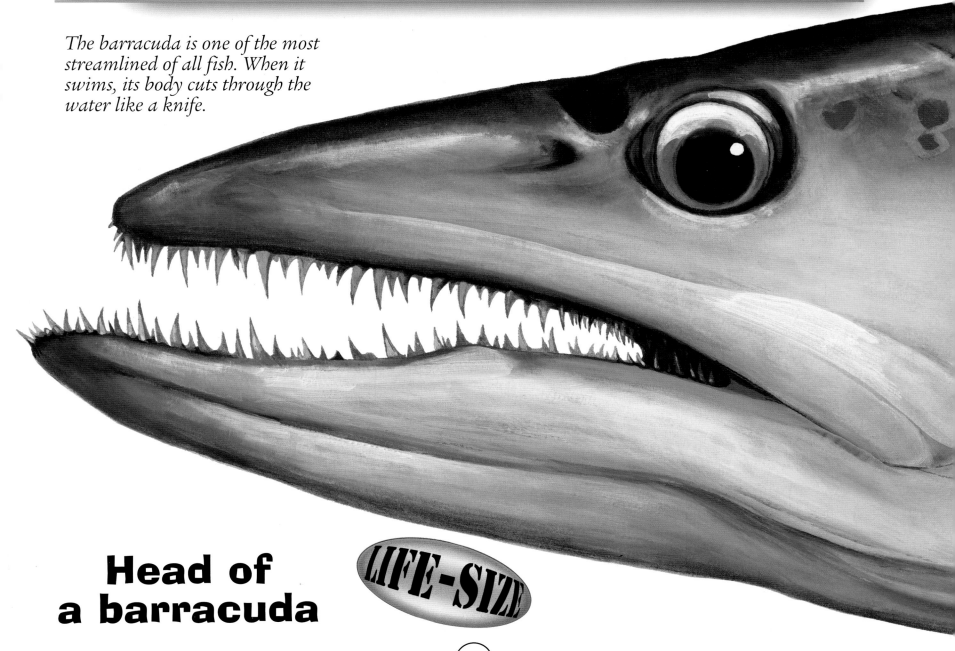

Head of a barracuda

LIFE-SIZE

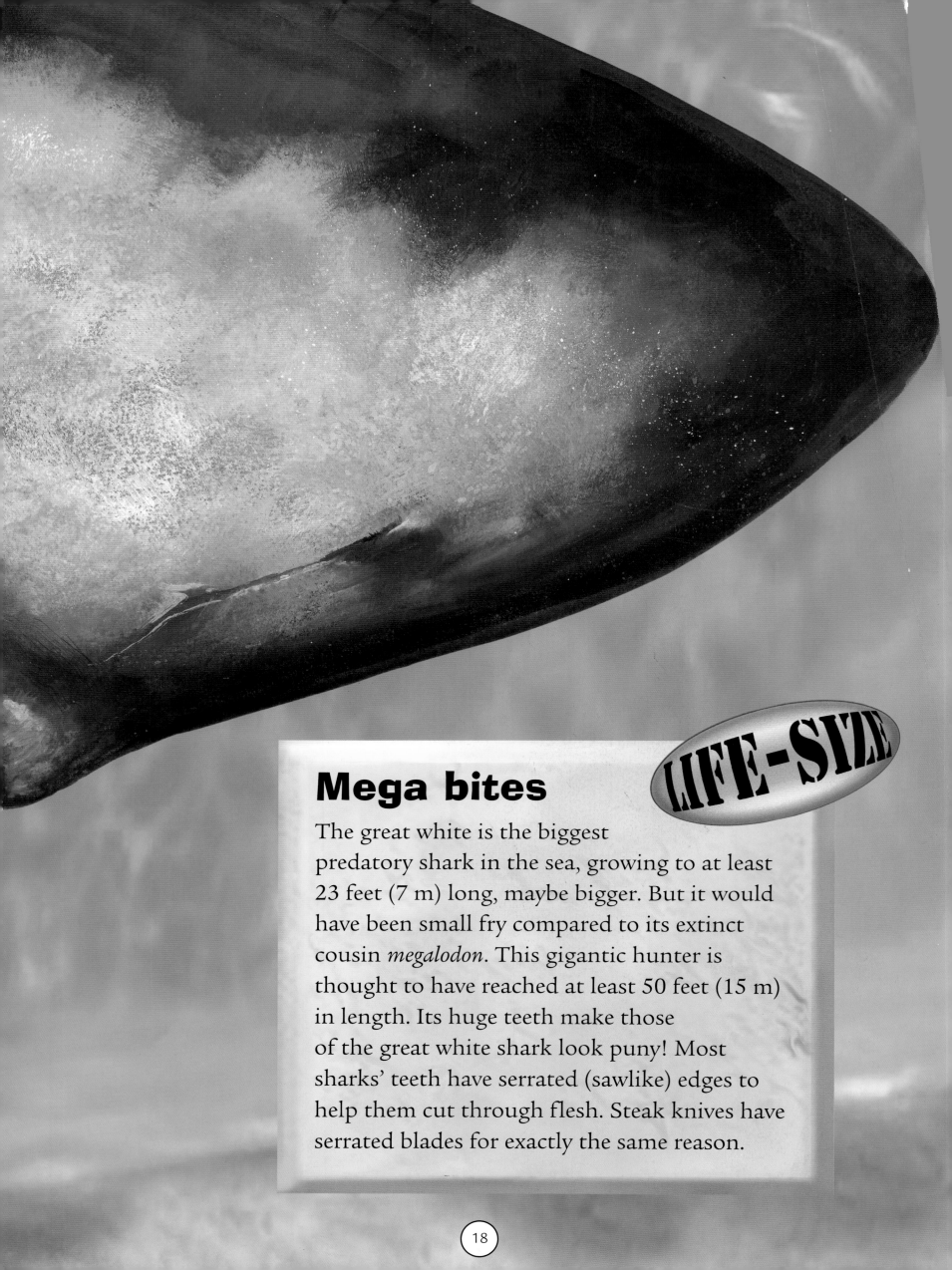

Mega bites

LIFE-SIZE

The great white is the biggest predatory shark in the sea, growing to at least 23 feet (7 m) long, maybe bigger. But it would have been small fry compared to its extinct cousin *megalodon*. This gigantic hunter is thought to have reached at least 50 feet (15 m) in length. Its huge teeth make those of the great white shark look puny! Most sharks' teeth have serrated (sawlike) edges to help them cut through flesh. Steak knives have serrated blades for exactly the same reason.

OTHER WAYS TO KILL PREY

LIFE-SIZE

Even the most unlikely creatures can be poisonous. The cone shell shoots its prey with a hollow spike, through which poison is injected.

A swift attack and powerful bite is just one way to kill prey. Many underwater creatures use less obvious methods. Some lie in wait for prey, hidden by camouflage. Others draw their victims toward their mouths by using bait.

Hidden dangers

Not all predators travel in search of prey, some wait for their victims to come to them. These are the ambush specialists—animals that stay hidden, waiting for the right moment to strike.

Most ambushers rely on camouflage to avoid being seen. They are colored, and sometimes even shaped, to match their surroundings. Stonefish, for instance, look almost exactly like the rocks on the seabed where they live. Their relatives, scorpionfish, are often colored to blend in with seaweed.

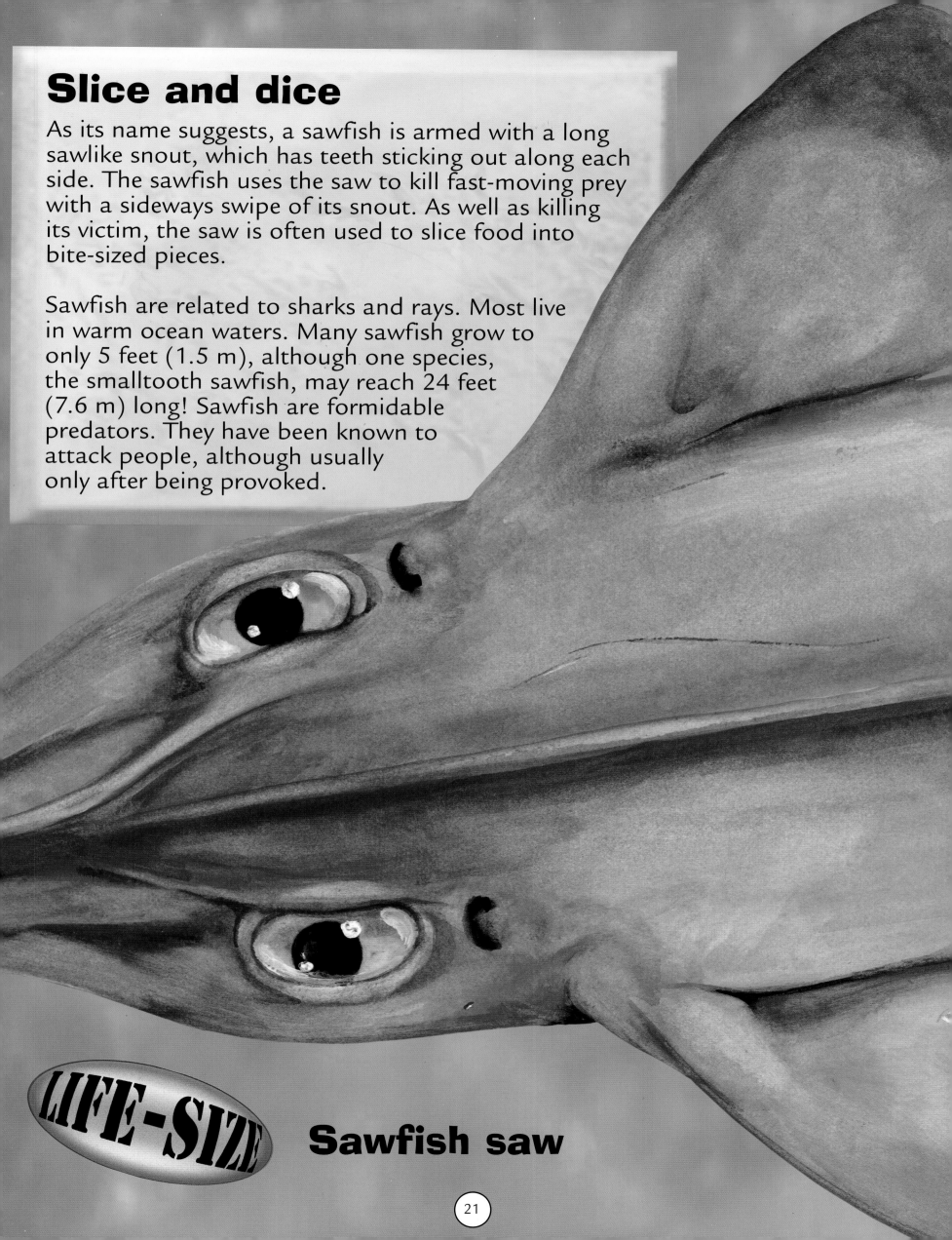

Slice and dice

As its name suggests, a sawfish is armed with a long sawlike snout, which has teeth sticking out along each side. The sawfish uses the saw to kill fast-moving prey with a sideways swipe of its snout. As well as killing its victim, the saw is often used to slice food into bite-sized pieces.

Sawfish are related to sharks and rays. Most live in warm ocean waters. Many sawfish grow to only 5 feet (1.5 m), although one species, the smalltooth sawfish, may reach 24 feet (7.6 m) long! Sawfish are formidable predators. They have been known to attack people, although usually only after being provoked.

LIFE-SIZE **Sawfish saw**

THE TWILIGHT ZONE

Between 500 and 2,300 feet (152 and 701 m) below the ocean's surface, the amount of light reaching through the water gradually fades. Known as the twilight zone, this habitat has its own unique animals, many unlike anything else on Earth.

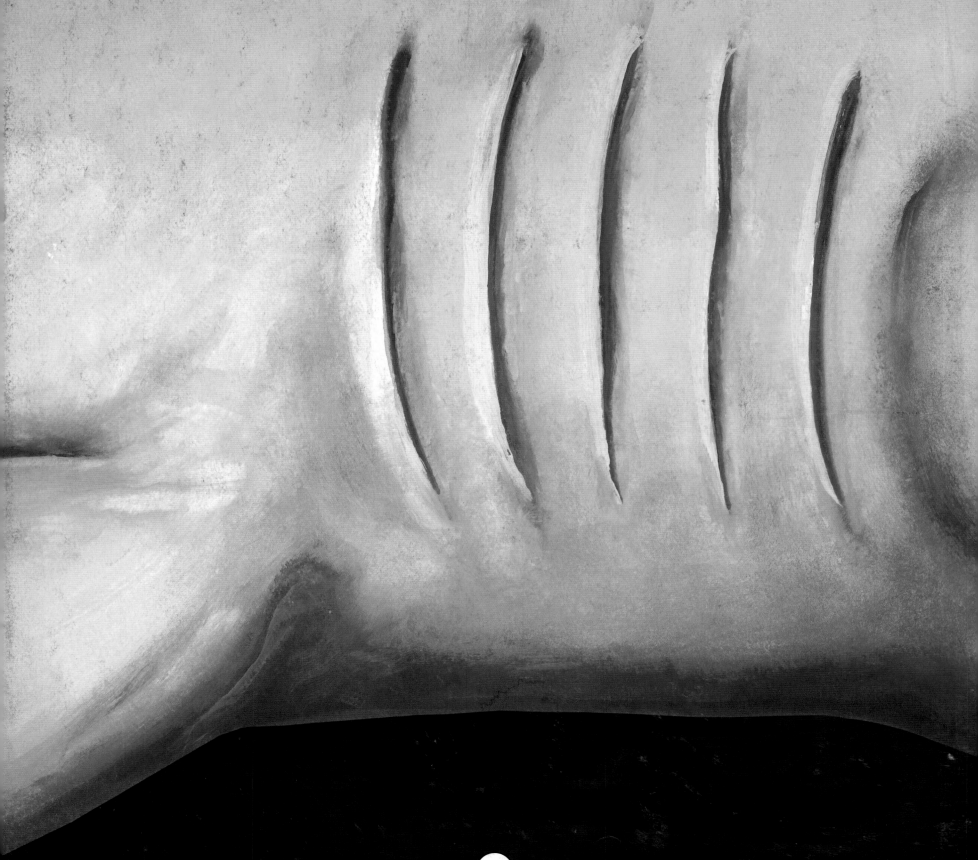

Glowing in the gloom

Very little sunshine reaches down into the twilight zone. But surprisingly this part of the ocean is sometimes lit with another type of light. Many twilight-zone animals are able to produce their own light. Some do this to tell mates where they are. Others do it to catch prey. Anglerfish, for example, have luminous lures to draw prey toward their mouths. There is even one fish that generates light for camouflage. Called the hatchet fish, it has two rows of lights on its belly, which match the color of sunlight coming down from above.

LIFE-SIZE

A fish makes a silhouette against the light shining down from the surface. The lights on a hatchet fish's belly fill in the silhouette, making the fish invisible.

This caridean shrimp is bright red because this color appears black in deep water, making it hard to see.

Fishing for food

Anglerfish use bait to attract their prey just like people do when they go fishing. But instead of a fishing rod, an anglerfish has a long spine that sticks out from its head. On the end of the spine is a fleshy lure that looks to many fish like a piece of food. The anglerfish twitches this lure to attract small fish into its large, toothy mouth. Anglerfish that live in deep and dark waters use lures that glow in the dark.

Anglerfish have fearsome teeth that are used to stab their prey and make sure it does not get away.

Twilight nightmare

Few fish look more frightening than the goblin shark. This bizarre bottom-dwelling monster has a face that would terrify even the toughest diver. Unlike other sharks, it has a long, flattened snout and jaws that it can push out of its mouth. This helps it to snap up prey quickly.

The goblin shark spends most of its time in the dark water near the seabed. Its tiny eyes see very little. However, the shark's long snout is equipped with electricity sensors that help it find prey on or even buried under the seabed. The goblin shark lives mostly in coastal waters where the seabed slopes gradually downward away from the shore. It hunts squid, fish and other creatures living near the sea bottom. The shark even catches crabs, crushing their shells in its back teeth. Male goblin sharks reach 12 ½ feet (3.8 m) long.

LIFE-SIZE

INTO THE ABYSS

Below 2,300 feet (700 m), the ocean is cold and completely dark. This forbidding place is the deep sea, and it is home to some of the weirdest and most scary-looking of all underwater creatures.

Drifting in darkness

Deep-sea animals inhabit a world without sunlight. Some live on the seabed, but many float freely in the still, dark water, never seeing and rarely feeling a solid surface.

Many free-swimming animals in the deep sea have soft, fragile bodies. Comb jellies, for instance, are more than nine-tenths water! Others have tougher but often still flexible bodies. The vampire squid, for example, has powerful muscles that can change its body shape at will.

Adult vampire squid have earlike fins, which they flap up and down to move themselves through the water.

Super senses

In the blackness of the deep sea, eyesight becomes unimportant and other senses take over. One of the most important of these is touch and the ability to sense vibrations and currents in the water. The hairy anglerfish has long, fleshy hairs covering its body. These pick up the slightest movement and direct the fish toward its prey.

Another important sense in the deep sea is smell. Sharks have a highly developed sense of smell. Deep-sea species, such as the bluntnose sixgill shark, use it to find the rotting bodies of dead animals that have sunk to the ocean floor.

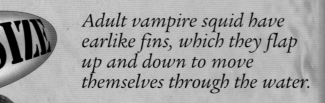

Hunting in the dark

Catching prey in complete darkness is very difficult. To improve their chances of hitting victims, many deep-sea predators have long, protruding teeth. The viperfish has some of the most frightening teeth of all. They stick out from its mouth like long, curved needles, ready to impale any creature that comes into reach.

Some deep-sea hunters have small teeth but huge mouths. One of the most extreme examples is the gulper eel. This 6-foot (1.8 m) animal has such a huge mouth that it hardy ever misses. Prey is snapped up in its pelicanlike jaws, which can unhinge to grab fish as big as the eel itself.

Staying out of sight

Animals living in open water have no place to hide. Many survive by keeping an eye out for danger and they make a very quick getaway when hunters approach.

Other sea animals, such as jellyfish and shrimp, avoid attacks by being transparent. What little light does come from above passes right through their bodies, making them almost invisible.

Viper fish

Like many deep-sea fish, the viper fish has a large stomach that can expand, allowing it to eat a lot whenever food is plentiful.

LIFE-SIZE

**Hammerhead
shark**

CORAL REEFS

Coral reefs are sometimes called the rainforests of the sea. Like rainforests, the reefs are home to a huge range of animals. The biodiversity of a coral reef is higher than any other part of the ocean. This means that more different types of plant and animal live here than anywhere else.

Bright and beautiful

Coral-reef fish are among the most colorful creatures on Earth. They come in nearly every color imaginable. Some are so bright that they almost glow. The reason for these rainbow colors is hard to understand. They certainly do not help the fish hide from predators! Scientists think that they might simply be a way for fish to identify others of their own kind in the crowded waters.

Coral-reef fish include angelfish and butterfly fish. Angelfish munch on sponges, while butterfly fish eat tiny worms and swimming animals.

LIFE-SIZE

Imperial angelfish

Forceps butterfly fish

How corals live

Corals are colonies of many small animals, known as polyps. Each polyp looks like a tiny sea anemone, with a ring of stinging tentacles around its mouth. Many coral polyps produce a hard, chalky case around their bodies to protect them from predators. The protective cases of polyps in colonies grow together to form beautiful structures. When a polyp dies, its skeleton is left behind, and a new polyp grows on top of it. Coral polyps are animals, but many have tiny plantlike algae living inside them. Whenever sunlight shines on these algae, they produce sugars, which they share with the polyp.

Over many thousands of years, the chalky cases left behind by coral polyps build up to produce the massive underwater structures we call coral reefs.

Living together

Some coral-reef creatures live in partnerships. Clownfish live among the tentacles of sea anemones, for example. The tentacles keep predators away from the clownfish. Slime on the fish's skin protects it from the anemone's stings.

The cleaner wrasse has a partnership with many types of coral-reef animal. Instead of attacking the little fish, they let it swim all over them, even into their mouths. The wrasse nips off parasites from the other creatures' bodies. (Parasites are animals that live on or inside the body of another animal.) Everyone benefits from this system. The larger fish get rid of their pests while the cleaner wrasse gets a meal.

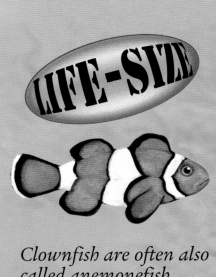

LIFE-SIZE

Clownfish are often also called anemonefish because of the way they live alongside large sea anemones.

Wide-eyed

The great hammerhead shark is one of the most deadly of all coral-reef hunters. With its huge mouth and razor-sharp teeth, this 20-foot (6 m) monster can make mincemeat of any animal it decides to attack.

Like all hammerheads, the great hammerhead has its eyes, nostrils and other sense organs wide apart. It may be that this helps the shark to find its prey. Having its eyes far apart might help the hammerhead judge distances better. Its nostrils are widely spaced too, and this could make it easier for the shark to detect in which direction a particular smell is coming from. As with all sharks, hammerheads can also sense the electricity produced by another animal's muscles. The hammer-shaped head also makes this sense more accurate.

OCEAN VOYAGERS

Compared to shallow, coastal waters, the open ocean is almost completely empty of life, like a desert on land. The few animals that do live out there have special adaptations to help them survive. Many of them travel across the open ocean on long journeys, known as migrations.

Going with the flow

Many open-ocean animals drift along with the current. Jellyfish move by pulsing their bell-shaped bodies, but they cannot swim very well. Instead, they travel wherever the ocean waters take them and catch food with stinging tentacles that trail below. Another ocean drifter is the Portuguese man-of-war. It is actually made up of hundreds of animals living together. Some of them form a large, air-filled float, which has a sail to catch the wind. Others make up stinging tentacles to trap prey and another group break down food.

The Portuguese man-of-war is blown along by the wind.

LIFE-SIZE

Sprint finishers

In the open ocean there is nowhere to hide. The fish that live here are fast swimmers and can see danger coming from a long way off. For predators to survive, they have to be even faster. Open-ocean predators include the quickest animals in the sea. The fastest swimmer of all is the cosmopolitan sailfish. This super-streamlined hunter can reach up to 68 miles per hour (109 kph) in short bursts. Other speedy ocean predators include the shortfin mako shark, which reaches speeds of 60 miles per hour (97 kph) and the marlin, which can swim at 50 miles per hour (81 kph).

The world's fastest swimmer, the cosmopolitan sailfish, grows to 10 feet (3 m) long.

Incredible journey

If it could speak, the common eel would have an amazing story to tell. Although it spends most of its life in the rivers and marshes of Europe, it was born thousands of miles away in the open ocean. When they become adults, common eels leave their freshwater homes and swim down to the sea. They then travel right across the Atlantic Ocean to an area east of the Caribbean, known as the Sargasso Sea. Here, they breed and lay their eggs at the bottom of deep ocean trenches. The adult eels then die, leaving their young to hatch and make the return journey alone.

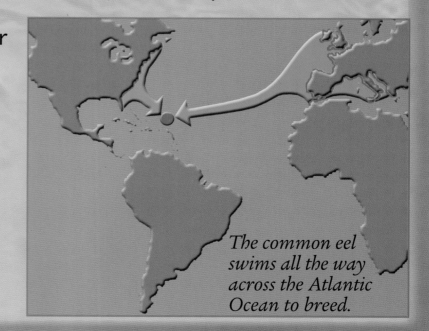

The common eel swims all the way across the Atlantic Ocean to breed.

The Kraken

Long ago, Vikings told tales of the Kraken. This mighty beast was like a floating island and had tentacles that could pull whole ships underwater. The Kraken was probably more than a myth. Its description matches the giant squid, a true monster that sometimes rises from the deep to swim at the surface. Vikings on the ocean at night may have seen this gigantic creature, which has tentacles 40 feet (12 m) long!

REAL-LIFE SEA MONSTERS

Many tales of sea monsters are based in fact, inspired by sightings of real-life animals. New finds keep adding to our list of monstrous sea creatures. It seems likely that many others might be out there, still waiting to be discovered.

Ancient accounts of real animals inspired stories of monsters. The creature above was drawn from a description of a sawfish.

Oarfish usually live in deep water, but they are occasionally seen swimming near the surface.

Sea serpents

Stories of sea serpents terrified early sailors. Some said that these enormous monsters would reach out and pluck men from the masts and rigging, or wrap their coils around entire ships and drag them under the water.

In truth neither of these things ever happened, but sailors probably did see real creatures they thought were sea serpents. The oarfish, for instance, could definitely be mistaken for a giant sea snake. Its long, slender body grows to a length of 56 feet (17 m).

The basking shark feeds on tiny animals near the surface. It may also bask in the sun on the surface of the water.

Modern sea monsters

Many other sea monsters of old were probably based on sailors seeing real animals, such as whales and sharks. As sailors told each other their stories, these sea creatures became more monstrous and terrifying. Today, we know much more about sea creatures than we did in the past. Seeing a basking shark or a whale shark, the two largest fish in the world, for example, would have struck fear into sailors many years ago. Instead of being ship-sinking monsters, we know today that these sharks are harmless filter-feeders.

The basking shark is about 30 feet (9 m) long and the whale shark grows to an even larger size. Both sharks often float, or bask, on the surface, forming a living island. They even let people walk up and down their backs.

Leviathans

The word *leviathan* is an ancient one. It appears in the Old Testament of the Bible and some even earlier writings. In medieval times, a leviathan was a particular type of giant monster that swam around ships to create whirlpools that sucked them and their crew underwater.

The legend of the leviathan was most probably inspired by sightings of whales. Humpback whales even behave a bit like these monsters, swimming in circles to create rings of bubbles. They use these bubbles to trap fish before bursting up through the middle to swallow their catch.

Humpback whales create 'nets' of bubbles to trap shoals of fish.

Giant-squid tentacles

LIFE-SIZE

BEACH INVADERS

Some sea creatures occasionally come out onto land. Most do this to lay eggs or give birth to their young, but a few actually feed along the shoreline. Many other types of animals that live in coastal waters become trapped in rock pools as the tide goes out.

Mudskipper males raise their dorsal (back) fins to warn rival males to stay away. They scan for danger with eyes that move independently of each other.

Fish out of water

Mudskippers spend much of their time on land. Like other fish, they have gills to breathe underwater, but they can also take oxygen in through their skin. Mudskippers live along muddy shores in warm regions, from Africa in the west through Asia to the South Pacific. They eat worms and other small creatures that live on the shore.

Mudskippers have adaptations to help them move about on land. Their front fins are strong enough to lift their bodies off the ground, and their muscular tails flick to help them "skip" along. The fish also have a sucker disc on the underside on the body, allowing them to cling to the trunks of mangrove trees, which grow in the shallows.

Coming ashore

Turtles spend most of their lives in the ocean. But every year, females gather to haul themselves onto sandy beaches to lay their eggs. The turtles usually come ashore in darkness. Sometimes hundreds of turtles will arrive on the same beach at one time, churning up the sand with their flippers as they dig pits to bury their eggs in.

Many other air-breathing creatures, such as penguins and seals, come ashore to breed, but, amazingly, there is one type of fish that does it too. Capelin surge up onto beaches with the waves at high tide. The females lay their eggs and the males fertilize them. Then all the adults die. A few weeks later, the baby capelin hatch in the sand. When the next high tide comes in, the baby fish swim out to sea.

Hawksbill turtles may lay 200 eggs at a time. Once they have emerged from the sand, the little hatchlings race down to the sea as fast as their flippers will carry them.

LIFE-SIZE

LIFE-SIZE

Rock pools

All sorts of animals end up in rock pools. As the tide comes in, many creatures that live in the sea come with it and stay behind when the tide goes out. The animals found in rock pools range from crabs and shrimp to sea slugs and small fish. A few, such as barnacles and sea anemones, may spend their whole lives there. Others escape into open water again as soon as they can.

In some parts of the world, rock pools hide dangerous animals. For example, people in Australia often find the small but deadly blue-ringed octopus in pools.

The beautiful but deadly blue-ringed octopus expands its rings as a warning to show that it is poisonous.

LIFE IN FRESH WATER

Freshwater habitats include rivers, lakes, ponds and swamps. The creatures that live there are different from those found in the seas and oceans. Many, however, are just as frightening, dangerous or weird.

Freshwater giants

Most of the world's biggest fish live in the oceans, but a few giants make their home in lakes or rivers. One of the largest freshwater fish is the arapaima, which lives in the Amazon and other South American rivers. It can weigh 440 pounds (200 kg) and reach more than 10 feet (3 m) long!

The alligator snapping turtle is another giant. This monstrous reptile is well named because it has a bite powerful enough to slice its prey in two. The alligator snapper entices fish toward its jaws by wiggling a wormlike lure in the bottom of its opened mouth. Lying in wait on the bottom of a swamp or river, the turtle can be surprisingly well hidden— alligator snappers move about so little that plants often grow on their shells.

The alligator snapper is the world's largest freshwater turtle. The biggest one ever recorded weighed 236 pounds (107 kg).

LIFE-SIZE

Some freshwater turtles grow no bigger than the palm of your hand.

Killer fish

Red-bellied piranhas have a bloodthirsty reputation. These South American fish can strip the flesh from a dead horse in minutes, leaving nothing but the skeleton behind.

Red-bellied piranhas live and feed in shoals. Once one attacks, the rest quickly follow. The shoal then goes into a feeding frenzy, leaving a victim little hope of escape. Individual red-bellied piranhas are quite small—just 12 inches (30 cm) long—but their shoals may be hundreds strong. These terrifying fish are armed with some of the sharpest teeth of any animal. The teeth are triangles with saw-toothed edges, like those of sharks.

The red-bellied piranha has a mouthful of razor-sharp teeth.

High voltage

Almost as famous as the red-bellied piranha is South America's electric eel. This river fish eats meat and some grow to 9 feet (2.7 m) long. It uses electricity to stun or kill its prey, firing off shocks of up to 650 volts! That is nearly three times what comes out of a plug at home.

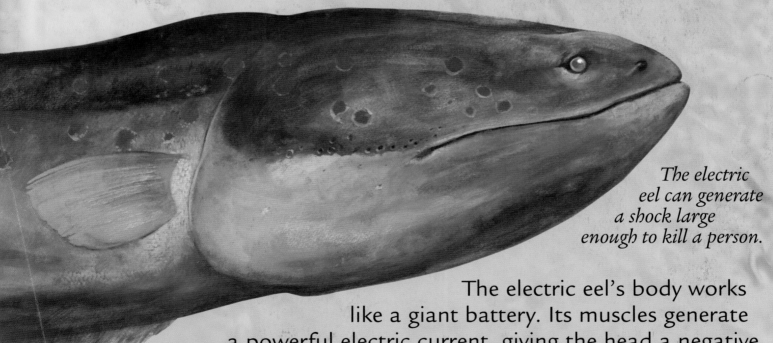

The electric eel can generate a shock large enough to kill a person.

The electric eel's body works like a giant battery. Its muscles generate a powerful electric current, giving the head a negative charge and the tail a positive one. The eel attacks prey by touching them with its head and tail end at the same time. This causes current to run through the prey's body, giving it a deadly electric shock.

Alligator snapping turtle

Like many large turtles and tortoises, this giant might live for at least 150 years!

INDEX